An
ABC
Reflections
Journal

Reflections of the Life Experiences and Lessons of a Mother, Grandmother, and Great-grandmother

SHARON ELAM

Olympus Story House
www.olympusstoryhouse.com

CONTENTS

Introduction — 1
Ability — 2
Beauty — 4
Communication — 6
Dreams/Desires of Our Hearts — 8
Eternity — 10
Forgiveness — 12
Freedom — 14
Growth — 16
Happiness — 18
Intuition — 20
Joy — 22
Kindness — 24
Love — 26
Memories — 28
Newness — 30
Optimism — 32
Peace — 34
Quality — 36
Rain — 38
Sunshine — 40
Tears — 42
Trust in the Lord — 44
Unity — 46
Variety — 48
Wisdom/Work — 50
X-Ray — 52
Yes — 54
Zeal/Zealot — 56
About the Author — 58

Because someone I love is in Heaven
There is a bit of Heaven in my heart.

Who You Are

(Dedicated to my daughter, Katie)
(Transitioned March 7, 2018)

Being Who You Are
Helps Me
To Be Who I Am…

Our journey may take us,
Side by side for a while.
And yet sometimes, our journey
May take each of us,
On different paths.

Though we walk not
Side by side
I still feel united
To you in spirit.

My love for you
Always goes with you
Along your path…
As I feel your love
Going with me along my path…

I know our paths
Will crisscross
From time to time
In order that we might
Reunite and share
Our experiences with each other
And rejoice at the beautiful person
God is calling each one of us to be…

To be fully human
To be fully alive
To be fully united in Christ Jesus
In the center of His most precious heart
Is my prayer for you…

Written
(11/5/87)

INTRODUCTION

Father in heaven,
The hand of your loving kindness
Powerfully yet gently guides all the
Moments of our day.
Go before us in our pilgrimage of life,
Anticipate our needs and prevent our falling.
Send your Spirit to unite us in faith,
That sharing in your service,
We may rejoice in your presence.
We ask this through Christ our Lord.

I am experienced in being brought low,
Yet I know what it is to have an abundance.
I have learned how to cope with every circumstance
How to eat well or go hungry,
To be well provided for or do without.

"In him who is the source of my strength
I have strength for everything."

"My God, in turn, will supply your needs fully,
In a way worthy of his magnificent riches in Christ Jesus."

"All glory to our God and father for unending ages!"
(Philippians 4:12-14, 19–20)

ABILITY

What are the abilities I possess?
Knowing my abilities has helped me develop into the person I have been called to be, and this is an ongoing process.
What are the gifts I have that others acknowledge in me?
Can I acknowledge these gifts within myself?
I have the power to choose or not to choose to develop my gifts.
My goal is to acknowledge, develop, and use my gifts in the service of others.
It is in giving yourself that you will find contentment.
Loving God and others is what each of us is called to do now and for all eternity.

I can do all things through Christ which strengthens me.
—Philippians 4:13

My thoughts:

____

____

____

____

____

____

____

____

____

____

____

____

____

____

____

____

____

BEAUTY

It has been said that beauty is in the eyes of the beholder.
To see the beauty in all things is a blessing from God,
And a gift we can share with each other.
Slowing down from our fast-paced life allows us to see all the beauty surrounding us.
To sit and *be* has many rewards.
Make time in your life to *be* in a quiet place to be yourself.
It is in the quiet times that we can hear,
The beauty of God's voice speaking to us.
He has a beautiful message for each one of us.
Stop, listen, and learn how God speaks to you
To each one of us, He speaks differently and in a unique way so we know it is Him.
His spirit is with us for all eternity and
He lives within our hearts.
His love comes from His heart to my heart.

Your beauty should not come from outward adornments, such
as braided hair and the wearing of gold jewelry and fine clothes.
Instead, it should be that of your inner self, the unfading beauty of
a gentle and quiet spirit, which is of great worth in God's sight.

—1 Peter 3:3–4

My thoughts:

COMMUNICATION

What are all of our ways to communicate?

We have unlimited ways:
Our voice—how do others hear my voice… loud, gentle, caring
Our eyes—do they show love, happiness, or concern…
Our arms—do they hug me… separate me from you… open to you.
Our hands—do they help others in need.
Our ears—do they help me to listen to you.
Our face—does it show me how you feel.
Our smile—does it show that I am happy to see you…
Our actions—do they affirm who I am to you.
Our silence—does it allow others to speak without interruption.
Our body language—does it show I am closed or open to you.
Our behaviors—are they respectful of your boundaries.
Our expressions—are they affirming and joyful.
Our walk—is it heavy or light.
Our singing—is it joyful and happy.
Our demeanor—does it tell you who I am and that I love you.

My dear brothers and sisters, take note of this: Everyone should
be quick to listen, slow to speak, and slow to become angry.
—James 1:19

My thoughts:

____

____

____

____

____

____

____

____

____

____

____

____

____

____

____

____

____

____

DREAMS/DESIRES OF OUR HEARTS

We all have dreams.

Some are spoken, and some are unspoken that live within us.

What do you dream about and desire for your life?

The question is: How can I achieve the dreams and desires of my heart?

What are the steps I need to take?

First, I must think about and realize what my dreams are.

Second, I must create a plan to accomplish and complete my dreams.

Next, I must commit to my plan and be open to the timetable to accomplish my dream.

Where does the desire of my heart come from?

It comes from God.

God's plan and purpose for our lives within us.

In my heart's quiet place and stillness, I will become aware of God's voice and direction for my life.

His hand is always upon us, guiding and directing our daily journey.

Be aware of His presence every day of our lives.

Seek Him above all else.

Enjoy the journey!

"For I know the plans I have for you," declares
the Lord, "plans to prosper you and not to harm
you, plans to give you hope and a future."
—Jeremiah 29:11

My thoughts:

____

____

____

____

____

____

____

____

____

____

____

____

____

____

____

____

____

____

ETERNITY

My eternity began at the moment of my conception.
My journey is from God to God.
I can make of my eternity what I will
By the choices I make.
Although I will stumble and fall
Or maybe I will try to blaze my own way.
But this I know.
That if I keep my eyes fixed on Jesus
The path that I am to follow will be revealed.
I need never fear for He is always with me.
When the going gets tough
I will remember
To refocus my eyes on Jesus.
He is the way, the truth, and life.
He is with whom I shall spend eternity.
I am only here as a part of the journey I am on,
Passing from this life into the next.
Behold, I stand at the door knocking…
Open yourself to me that we may be one,
For now and all eternity.

For God so loved the world, that He gave His only begotten Son, that whoever believes in Him shall not perish, but have *eternal* life.

—1 John 5:12

My thoughts:

____

____

____

____

____

____

____

____

____

____

____

____

____

____

____

____

____

____

____

FORGIVENESS

What is forgiveness?
Does forgiveness have a positive effect on my life?
What is the positive side of forgiveness for me?
Who benefits from my forgiveness?
Forgiveness is a process.
A process with lasting benefits
Forgiveness sets us free to heal.
Forgiveness opens the doors so I can move on in my life's journey.
Forgiveness clears the way for me to love others unconditionally.
Forgiveness frees me from the judgment of others.
Forgiveness lightens the load I carry on my shoulders.
Forgiveness lightens my footsteps so I can be playful and love freely.
Forgiveness helps me to be more open to God's movement and direction in my life.
My forgiveness inspires others to do the same.
Forgiveness is a choice I make.
Forgiveness has a powerful effect on my life and sets me free.
Forgiveness opens my heart to be able to love more.
Forgiveness opens my heart to be able to forgive myself.
Forgiveness fills my heart with peace.
God forgives and is always there for us. All we have to do is ask for it, and it is done, and the slate is wiped clean and forgotten forever.

Be kind and compassionate to one another, forgiving
each other, just as in Christ God forgave you.
—Ephesians 4:32

My thoughts:

FREEDOM

Freedom is knowing God has everything under control.
Freedom is not having to be in control.
Freedom is knowing God knows my needs better than I know my own.
Freedom is a *total surrender* to God.
Freedom is letting go and choosing God's will for my life.
Freedom is knowing God and living in His presence.
Freedom is living in the now moment.
Freedom is knowing God forgives me and sets me free.
Freedom is seeing God in the beauty of all creation.
Freedom is saying, "Here I Am Lord."
Freedom is being who God is calling me to be for all eternity.

Now the Lord is the Spirit, and where the
Spirit of the Lord is, there is freedom.

—1 Peter 2:16

My thoughts:

____

____

____

____

____

____

____

____

____

____

____

____

____

____

____

____

____

____

GROWTH

Growth comes in spurts.

Each period of growth needs to be integrated into our daily lives.

Each period of growth must be completed for our next period of growth to start.

Growth is not always easy. Remember to look for the positive side to every negative situation.

Some of the most significant periods of growth can come from our most painful experiences. Pain is our greatest teacher, and without pain, there is no growth.

What we learn about ourselves and others during painful experiences can profoundly affect our lives and how we see life.

Having a growth mindset is a way of viewing challenges and setbacks. People who have a growth mindset believe that even if they struggle with specific skills, their abilities aren't set in stone.

Why is a growth mindset so powerful?

We start learning in the womb and continue to grow for the rest of our lives. We are never "grown up," as some think that this is a goal we must achieve. The good news is that we do mature over the years. What used to bother us no longer bothers us… This is called mellowing out.

With a growth mindset, you know that you can change over time; therefore, you are more open to reflecting, learning, and growing from the challenges you face in your daily life.

Having a growth mindset is all about the attitude with which you face your challenges and how you process failures and adapt and evolve as a result.

Life experiences are your best teachers. Allow each experience to help you grow to be the person you are called to be. Be the best version of yourself.

Look for the good in every situation, seek the valuable *life lesson* in every setback, and look for the solution to every problem. Think and talk continually about your goals.

Remember: There are no failures… just learning experiences!

That I might know the greatness of His power in me.

—Ephesians 1:19

My thoughts:

HAPPINESS

Happiness and wholeness are a state of consciousness and are not "out there" to be acquired. Go within to find it.

Happiness protects your heart.

Happiness is knowing God looks at and smiles at me.

Happiness is knowing God laughs with me.

Happiness is knowing God is always with me.

Happiness is knowing God is always available to me.

Happiness is knowing God's plan and purpose for my life is perfect.

Happiness is knowing God enjoys watching me grow and develop.

Happiness is knowing God blesses me every day.

Happiness is knowing God's abundance surrounds me.

Happiness is knowing God will always provide for me.

Happiness is knowing God's protection is always around me.

Happiness is simply knowing and developing a relationship with God!

Delight yourself in the Lord, and He will
give you the desires of your heart.

—Psalm 37:4

My thoughts:

INTUITION

We are all blessed with this ability.

Intuition is the ability to know or understand through your feelings instead of by considering facts or evidence.

It is the ability to use good judgment and make sensible, common-sense decisions based on your knowledge and experiences.

Intuition is a feeling in your gut or inner voice where you instinctively know that something you are doing is right or wrong.

Intuition is a "light bulb" moment when you understand something or get a good idea out of nowhere.

Trust the process and learn from lessons drawn on your past experiences of not listening; this will improve your decision-making. What does it feel like?

It is a calm, inner knowing. If it doesn't work out, it is not the end of the world. It is growth-oriented in your body.

Your gut feeling is a sign of direction from the spirit of God that lives within each one of us.

Call on that Spirit to guide you for all the decisions you need to make.

When the Spirit of truth comes, he will guide you into all the truth,
for he will not speak on his own authority, but whatever he hears, he
will speak, and he will declare to you the things that are to come.

—John 16:13

My thoughts:

JOY

> Find your joy in God and rely on Him for strength.
> —Nehemiah 8:10

The joy that comes with the presence of the Lord is a joy that cannot be taken away from us.

Joy is a feeling of great pleasure, happiness, and well-being. It puts a smile on your face and in your heart because we have confidence in God.

We delight in His presence and anticipate that God will do something good.

Real joy is a byproduct of having a strong and intimate relationship with God.

At its very root, joy is a supernatural gift from God granting you peace that your life is right with God.

How do you feel joy in the Lord?
1. Discover the Lord's purpose for You. You are more than ordinary.
2. Find joy in your circumstances. One of the keys to finding joy is to recognize God's hand in your life, even during challenging moments…
3. Remember that joy multiplies.
4. Look for God in the ordinary and simple.

> May the God of hope fill you with all joy and peace in believing, so that by the power of the Holy Spirit you may abound in hope. (Romans 15:13)

Be joyful in your hope. Be patient in times
of affliction. Persevere in prayer.

—Romans 12:12

My thoughts:

KINDNESS

Kindness is more than behavior.

Kindness means having a spirit of helpfulness, being generous and considerate, and doing so without expecting anything in return.

Kindness is a quality of being. It will lift your spirits to be of assistance to someone.

Kindness can mean different things to different people. The meaning is in how *you* choose to show it. Be it through empathy, acceptance, kind gestures, and thoughtfulness, the possibilities are entirely up to you.

It is not just how you treat others but how you also extend those same behaviors and intentions to yourself.

Random acts of kindness are good for your heart and soul.

For example, in a drive-through, pay for the car behind you. It will make your day.

Bring your chiropractor a plate of homemade cookies. It will make them smile and let them know someone cares about them.

Has someone ever done something kind to you and all you wanted to do after was pay it forward? That's because kindness is a chain reaction. It's a wave that keeps rolling; all it needs is one person to start it.

One small act of kindness can cause a ripple effect, impacting an entire community. We create a change movement if we are all focused on being kind.

Do you know that famous "be the change you wish the see in the world" quote? That quote isn't just about change; it isn't only about one person being able to change their world. It's more extensive; it is about a movement that can be started by one person acting with intention.

When you see someone being kind or notice it from a family member or friend, tell them you appreciate what they did. Positive reinforcement helps people want to do more good deeds and reminds people to act with intention.

Now continue to be kind and change the world.

Be kind and compassionate to one another, forgiving
each other, just as in Christ, God forgave you.
—Ephesians 4:32

My thoughts:

LOVE

Love is the essence of who we are and lives within our hearts.

This love is God Himself, who has created each one of us.

Since He lives within us, He is always available to us, and we can turn to Him at any moment of any day or night.

Thank You, Lord, for always being there for us. May Your presence reign in our lives.

In 1 Corinthians 13:4–8a (ESV), "Love is patient and kind; love does not envy or boast; it is not arrogant or rude. It does not insist on its own way; it is not irritable or resentful; it does not rejoice at wrongdoing but rejoices with the truth."

What does true love look like?

A truly loving relationship should have communication, affec-tion, trust, appreciation, and mutual respect. If you see these signs and the relationship is a healthy, honest, nurturing one, you will likely consider your relationship one of true love.

Love must be nurtured and worked on daily for growth to happen.

A stagnant relationship without daily nurturing will wither and die.

Expressing love daily nurtures a relationship with new growth and deeper understanding.

A motto to live by: I stand fully responsible for all my words and actions.

Our sole purpose in life is to love one another!

Love heals everything!

If it isn't love, it isn't real!

Above all, clothe yourselves with love, which binds us all together in perfect harmony. And regardless of what else you put on, wear love. It's your basic, all-purpose garment. Never be without it.

—Colossians 3:12–14

My thoughts:

MEMORIES

Memories are ours to treasure. They can never be taken away from us and are held in a sacred place in our hearts and minds.

What a gift we have in this ability to remember.

Some of our memories are happy and joyful, and others are not, but each can be a tremendous learning experience.

Each of us has different memories and perceptions of a given situation. What triggers a memory is different for each of us.

It may be a song we hear or something someone says to us. It could also be a situation where we find ourselves in.

How we respond is different for each of us and serves a partic-ular purpose.

It is okay to express the feelings that surface at these times. Feelings are a means of healing and growth. They teach us so much about ourselves and help us to become the person we are called to be.

Embrace the process and know all is well. Trust yourself and your intuition to guide and direct you through your life.

Look for signs that show you the path you are to follow. Ask God to open the doors that need to be opened and close the doors that need to be closed to keep you in the center of His perfect will for you.

Ask Him to execute His plan for you every day upon your arising.

Then trust the process and happenings of each day.

But the Helper, the Holy Spirit, whom the Father will
send in My name, He will teach you all things, and
bring to your remembrance all that I said to you.

—John 14:26

My thoughts:

____

____

____

____

____

____

____

____

____

____

____

____

____

____

____

____

____

NEWNESS

Behold, I make all things new.
What are the fruits of newness?
The fruits of newness are love, joy, and peace.

> The fruit of the Spirit is love, joy, peace, patience, kindness, goodness, faithfulness, gentleness, and self-control. (Galatians 5:22–26)

Each day is a new beginning. We live moment to moment.
Yesterday is gone. Tomorrow is not here yet.
Walk in the "newness of life" each day.
It is an abundant life, one that we can look back upon and say that it was worth it. It was worth it all.
Newness has a soft and tender spirit, a humble evaluation of one's worth, and a heartfelt knowledge of one's helplessness and need of the Lord.
Look around and see each new day as an opportunity to grow and experience new situations.
Take the time to look at both sides of any given situation and see how every negative can be turned into a positive growth experience.

Those who trust in the Lord will renew their strength;
they will soar on wings like eagles; they will run and
not grow weary; they will walk and not faint.

—Isaiah 40:31

My thoughts:

OPTIMISM

What is an optimist?

An optimist is someone who always sees the bright side of any situation.

How do you look at life's situations?

I believe there is a positive side to any circumstance we encounter. We have to be objective and look for it.

Maybe the positive is only to learn we don't want to do something again that ends up being harmful. We can learn so much from our mistakes; they will sometimes be our most extensive growth experiences.

Optimism is a hopeful, positive outlook on the future, yourself, and the world around you. It is a vital part of resilience, the inner strength that helps you overcome tough times. Optimism will help you see, feel, and think positively.

Optimism helps you believe your hard work has a purpose and is a great motivation source.

The Optimist Creed
Promise Yourself

To be *so strong* that nothing can disturb your peace of mind. To talk health, happiness, and prosperity to every person you meet. To make all your friends feel that there is something in them. To look at the sunny side of everything and make your optimism come true. To think only of the best, to work only for the best, and to expect only the best. To be just as enthusiastic about the success of others as you are about your own. To forget the past mistakes and press on to the *greater achievements* of the future. Wear a cheerful countenance *at all times* and give every living creature you meet a smile. To give so much time to the improvement of yourself that you have *no time* to criticize others. To be too large for worry, too noble for anger, too strong for fear, and too happy to permit the presence of trouble. (Optimist International) *You can do it!*

"For I know the plans I have for you," declares
the Lord, "plans to prosper you and not to harm
you, plans to give you hope and a future."
—Jeremiah 29:11

My thoughts:

PEACE

What is peace?
Peace is knowing God is in control.
Peace is a deep abiding faith in God.
Peace is knowing God only wants what is best for me.
Peace is knowing God loves me unconditionally.
Peace is knowing I have God's protection around me at all times.
Peace is knowing God hears my prayers.
Peace is knowing God answers my prayers in the best way for me.
Peace is knowing God is available 24/7.
Peace is knowing God will provide all of my needs.
Peace is knowing God forgives me.
Peace is connecting with God within the stillness of my heart.
Peace is knowing "all is well within my soul."

Now may the Lord of peace himself give you peace at
all times in every way. The Lord be with you all."
—2 Thessalonians 3:16

My thoughts:

____

____

____

____

____

____

____

____

____

____

____

____

____

____

____

____

____

____

____

QUALITY

What is quality?
When I think about quality, the following synonyms come to mind.

Enjoyable—am I fun to be around and have a good sense of humor?
Pleasant—am I in a good mood and seeing the positive side?
Interesting—am I attractive and amusing to be around?
Nice—am I friendly and approachable?
Delightful—am I entertaining and congenial?
Agreeable—am I accommodating and likable?
Pleasing—am I charming and enjoyable to be around?
Virtuous—am I ethical and moral in my dealings with others?
Honest—am I straightforward and truthful?
Upstanding—am I a good and honorable person?
Reliable—can I be counted on to follow through on commitments?
Decent—am I authentic and fair in my dealings with others?
Noble—am I honorable and generous?
Wholesome—am I balanced and uplifting by my example?

Working on all these characteristics will help you be the best version of yourself.
Remember you are one of God's masterpieces!

But all things, when their true quality is seen, are made clear
by the light: because everything which is made clear is light.
—Ephesians 5:13

My thoughts:

RAIN

Perhaps deep within us is the knowledge that rain is life itself, and all our emotions towards it are us being grateful that it pours.
Without water, there is no life.
Have you ever taken the time to go outside after it rains and smell the air?
Rain has such a clean and refreshing smell.
Rain waters the earth and gives vegetation a big drink of water and a free shower.
Your car gets a free car wash in the rain.
I love the sound of rain on the roof when I sleep.
Rain creates puddles for little children to splash in and laugh at.
Rain showers my spirit and waters my soul. (Emily Logan Deccens)

And I will make them and the places all around my
hill a blessing, and I will send down the showers in
their season; they shall be showers of blessings.
—Ezekiel 34:26

My thoughts:

SUNSHINE

Your smile is magical.
May sunshine always be around you each new day.
May smiles and love never be far away from you.
What does sunshine mean to you?
For me:
A good laugh brings sunshine to a home.
A bright day is ahead.
The flowers are blooming.
The air is warm on my face.
Even when it is raining, the sunshine is still there.
Sunshine brings brightness to our lives.
Children bring us laughter, so laugh and smile with them.
Learning is like sunshine to us. It helps us to grow, develop, and mature.
When I spend time with you, my world is so bright. You bring sunshine and light into my day.
When you can't seem to find the sunshine, *be* the sunshine. The name of the Lord is to be praised from the sun's rising to its setting.
Smile, God *loves you!*

The Lord bless you and keep you; the Lord make his
face shine on you and be gracious to you; the Lord
turn his face toward you and give you peace.

—Numbers 6:24–26

My thoughts:

TEARS

Tears have so many different meanings in our lives.
There are tears of joy.
There are tears of sadness.
There are tears of deep healing that we experience in the depths of our souls.
We cry for a variety of reasons.
Your emotions can cause you to cry when you're sad, angry, or happy. Each person is different.
Tears help us to relieve pent-up emotions and feelings.
We shed tears when a circumstance deeply moves us or what we may see.
All of the expressions of our tears have a purpose.
A person who cries is in touch with their emotions and is compassionate.
Remember it is *okay* to cry!

He will wipe away every tear from their eyes, and death shall
be no more, neither shall there be mourning, nor crying, nor
pain anymore, for the former things have passed away.
—Revelation 21:4

My thoughts:

TRUST IN THE LORD

"Trust the plan I have for you.
It will not be revealed to you before it happens.
Know that you are in a time of preparation.
Use this time to grow and be strong in your faith and trust in Me.
I will show you the way in my timing."

"Stay tuned to My voice.
I speak to you all day long in the people you meet,
The birds that you hear and the gentle breeze that blows.
I am everywhere—look for Me.
I am always with you.
My Mother is with me.
Speak to her about your loneliness.
She understands as I do."

"We will be there all the days of your life.
You are important to us.
I love you, my precious child.
Spend time with Me before the Blessed Sacrament.
I will do tremendous healing for you during this time.
I will keep you close to my Sacred Heart.
I, too, am left alone in the tabernacle.
Come to Me…
I love you, Sharon.
You are My Rose of Sharon.
Look for and see the joyful events in your life.
Be thankful for the healings that have taken place in your life."

Now may God, the inspiration and fountain of hope, fill you to overflowing with uncontainable joy and perfect peace as you trust in him. And may the power of the Holy Spirit continually surround your life with his super-abundance until you radiate with hope!

—Revelation 21:4

My thoughts:

UNITY

Our unity with God is our primary goal in life. United with Him, we can grow and become the person He calls each of us to be, and the result will be the best version of who we are.

The unity of the family is a precious gift. We have chosen to be in the family we are in and to learn the lessons we are here to complete and accomplish.

Sometimes unity is hard to maintain and has to be worked on. It's a work in progress in our daily lives.

Unity entails being open to other peoples' points of view without criticism.

Learning to listen is a gift we give to each other. Respect the speaker without interruption until they are finished speaking.

Unity keeps us close to each other and accepts others for who they are and not what we want them to be.

We are all individuals with unique gifts to share.

Unity binds us with God's love for us and each other.

I appeal to you, brothers and sisters, in the name of our
Lord Jesus Christ, that all of you agree with one another in
what you say and that there be no divisions among you,
but that you be perfectly united in mind and thought.

—1 Corinthians 1:10

My thoughts:

VARIETY

Variety has been called the spice of life and gives life all its flavor.
Life would certainly be boring without variety.
Variety is not getting stuck in doing the same thing every day the same way.
Explore different possibilities. There might be a better way to do something.
Variety brings colors into our lives. Remember all the colors in your crayon box?
How many different colors do you see each day, and what do they represent to you?
Exploring new things and learning new things keeps us stimulated by various activities.
Let your curiosity and creativity develop.
Do something you didn't think you could do. Your untapped abilities will amaze you and put a big smile on your face. Wow, I can do it, and I can do it!

Now there are varieties of gifts, but the same Spirit. And there are varieties of ministries and the same Lord. There are varieties of effects, but the same God who works all things in all persons.

—1 Corinthians 12:4–6

My thoughts:

____

____

____

____

____

____

____

____

____

____

____

____

____

____

____

____

____

____

____

WISDOM/WORK

Our life experiences give us wisdom.

Some experiences are positive, and some are negative, but each provides us with a learning experience.

Sometimes we learn, "Well, I am not going to do that again!"

It is wise for us to tap into our elders' wisdom and experiences and the knowledge they have acquired. They have many stories to tell and are entertaining to listen to.

Most of our elders like to talk and share what they have learned throughout their lives. You will be surprised at what they know and are waiting to be asked to share.

My life journey, lessons, and experiences are expressed in this book you are now reading.

Remember how much I love you as you read these pages.

Learn from my experiences and live a positive life full of gratefulness and love.

If any of you lacks wisdom, he should ask God, who gives generously
to all without finding fault, and it will be given to him.

—James 1:5

My thoughts:

____
____
____
____
____
____
____
____
____
____
____
____
____
____
____
____
____
____
____

X-RAY

X-rays help us see what is not visible to the naked eye in our bodies. There are different kinds of X-rays, and they are used in the medical field for information about our bodies.

There is also another kind of X-ray: looking inside ourselves for information.

We need to explore what is inside us and our soul's connection to God. He lives within each one of us and guides our daily lives.

He speaks to us from within in the silence of our minds. He speaks to us, and we can learn to listen to His voice.

He speaks to us in our thoughts and answers our questions if we ask for His guidance.

His voice will become more familiar the more we listen to it.

It is wise to ask God before we make a decision: "Is this decision for my highest good?" Then wait for His answer, which will come in your thoughts.

My prayer has been, "Lord, open the doors that need to be opened and close the doors that need to be closed to keep me in the center of Your perfect will and plan for my life."

He will show you the way. Be open to His direction and follow it. You won't be sorry but grateful that you did.

Man looks at the outward appearance,
but the Lord looks at the heart.

—1 Samuel 16:7

My thoughts:

YES

Yes, is a very old word.

What a powerful word yes can be.

Noah said *yes* when God asked him to build the ark. Abraham said *yes* when God asked him to sacrifice his only son. Joseph said *yes* when God asked him to forgive his brothers who beat and sold him into slavery. Moses said *yes* when God told him to go to Pharaoh and ask him to let the Israelites go.

Saying yes to God and His plan for our lives will keep us on the journey that God has planned for us and is for our greatest good.

God will allow you to experience challenges to teach you important lessons and help make you a better person. But God will always answer your prayers because of His never-ending love for you and all of His children.

Sometimes we pray, and God grants us the desires of our hearts. But sometimes He simply says *no* or *wait*. It doesn't mean that what you're praying for isn't good. But God's ways are higher than ours. It's easy to become frustrated when God doesn't answer your prayer the way you wish He would.

God says no or wait because He has a greater purpose. Everything that happens is under His control (Job 42:2). This means that He doesn't make any mistakes. You will never know the cost of what you want. God may be sparing you from unforeseen trials that wouldn't be right for you in the future.

In His infinite wisdom, His answer to prayer is always perfect.

What is God asking you to say yes to?

By continually saying *yes* when God asks if we will go, serve, be, or love—each of us gets to be a part of the working of the Holy Spirit in the world. It is in these moments that we find the opportunity to surrender ourselves fully to Him and embrace the freedom that God has already extended.

Yes, my soul, find rest in God; my hope comes from him.
Truly, he is my rock and my salvation; he is my fortress; I will
not be shaken. My salvation and my honor depend on God;
he is my mighty rock, my refuge. Trust in him at all times, you
people; pour out your hearts to him, for God is our refuge.

—Psalm 62:5–8

My thoughts:

ZEAL/ZEALOT

Zeal is dedication or enthusiasm for something. If you have zeal, you're willing, energized, and motivated. Zeal is often used in a religious sense, meaning devotion to God or another religious cause. Zeal in Christianity is a burning desire to please God, to do His will, and to advance His glory in the world in every possible way. It is a desire which is not natural to men or women. It is a desire that the Spirit puts in the heart of every believer when they are converted to Christ.

How can I improve my zeal?
Eight powerful tips:

1. Stay around people who bring out the best in you and don't stress you out.
2. Be a warrior, not a worrier; take action.
3. Keep saying this to yourself: "You are stronger than this."
4. Always remember that "this, too, shall pass."
5. Find a way or build one.
6. The only person who can defeat you is yourself.
7. It is not the length but the depth of life that matters.
8. Embrace the process.

Approach your life challenges with zeal, that is, with great energy and enthusiasm. It will be worth the effort, and the rewards will be amazing.

Never be lacking in zeal, but keep your
spiritual fervor, serving the Lord.

—Romans 12:13

My thoughts:

____

ABOUT THE AUTHOR

Sharon Elam has dedicated over thirty years of her life to the profession of teaching.

Throughout her career, she touched the lives of countless students from diverse age groups, ranging from enthusiastic kindergartners to two-year community college students.

A love of learning has been a driving force in Sharon's life for herself and her students.

This passion for knowledge constantly motivates her to seek and uncover the positive side of every learning experience.

She firmly believes that education is a lifelong journey and the quest for knowledge never ends.

Though Sharon has retired from formal teaching, her enthusi-asm for education remains undiminished.

Her most remarkable joy now comes from watching her four great-grandchildren embark on their own lifelong learning journeys.

Each step of their development brings her immense happiness, as she knows that they are laying the foundations for a bright and promising future.

Throughout her life, Sharon has held a deep faith and belief in God. This spiritual foundation has guided her actions, instilling in her a sense of gratitude and humility.

May God's blessings and protection always be with us.